MW01102265

PLAIN JANE
WORKS OUT

A modified, simplified program
for fitness, health, and energy
designed to last a day and a half.

No Effort
    No "Burn"
        No Sweat
            No Results

The Official Publicity Photograph of the models in this book. Clockwise from the leopard leotard at the top of the page: Arleen Sorkin, Tracey Berg, Linda Sunshine, Cassandra Danz and Mary Fulham.

PLAIN JANE WORKS OUT

by Linda Sunshine

With photographs by Martin Jackson

Featuring The High-Heeled Women:
Cassandra Danz
Tracey Berg
Mary Fulham
Arleen Sorkin

BANTAM BOOKS
TORONTO · NEW YORK · LONDON · SYDNEY

For my sister, Susan Sunshine Dorenter

Special thanks to CFM, BJ, Ken Sansone, Barry Denenberg, Brad Miner, Linda Grey, Jack Romanos, Ella and Sarah Stewart, Walter and Sam Brett, Kiki Bridges, Ellen Pavelka, HRR, Sharon Lerner, Emily Chewning, Sandra Glasser and the utterly *fabulous* High-Heeled Women—Cassandra, Tracey Arleen and Mary.

PLAIN JANE WORKS OUT
A Bantam Book/May 1983

Plain Jane is a trademark of Linda Sunshine

ISBN 0-553-34037-9

Published simultaneously in the United States and Canada

Bantam Books are published by Bantam Books, Inc. Its trademark,
consisting of the words "Bantam Books" and the portrayal of a
rooster is Registered in U.S. Patent and Trademark Office and in
other countries. Marca Registrada. Bantam Books, Inc., 666 Fifth
Avenue, New York, New York, 10103.

PRINTED IN THE UNITED STATES OF AMERICA
0 9 8 7 6 5 4 3 2 1

Dedicated to my mother
—who made me eat everything on my plate—
and then told me to go on a diet.

Contents

Prologue

Like a great many women, I've tried hard to look like Jane Fonda. I bought her workout record. I bought her video tape. I even bought a red-and-black-striped leotard.

I went to work. I "did Jane Fonda" every day, sometimes twice a day. Once, I even attempted Rover's Revenge. And, yes, I felt the burn.

After a few months, I looked in the mirror and what did I see? Barbarella? Bree Daniels? Chelsea Thayer? No, just me, Plain Jane.

But I didn't get angry, I got even.

I sat down and wrote my own exercise book.

I admit to borrowing freely from the Other Jane. Basically, I have transformed her ridiculously strenuous workout into something that's just plain easy to do.

Plain Jane Works Out is the perfect exercise plan for every woman who knows she'll never have thighs like Jane Fonda, so why bother?

Relax, sit back, enjoy. Exercise is easy when you learn not to sweat it.

Plain Jane

Plain Jane Shapes Up

My very favorite outdoor sport is going to the movies.

As a child, I was not very athletic. I did not like to participate in games. In fact, my only outdoor activity was chasing the Good Humor truck down the street.

When I grew up, I moved to New York City where it was even easier to forget about exercising. In Manhattan, I get my daily dose of fresh air by opening the window of my taxi cab. (I prefer the big Checker cabs; they remind me of the great outdoors.) Although I have advanced from chasing ice cream trucks to hailing cabs, my earlier training has served me well.

In the late 1970s, I noticed the alarming tendency of all my friends to exercise regularly. Suddenly, I was the only one without a sport. I did not want to be left out so I began my search for an exercise routine. It was time for Plain Jane to shape up.

I began with **BALLET.** I signed up for ten beginner classes at the Joffrey School of Ballet (Adult-After-Work-Not-Really-Serious-Dancers Division).

My first problem was those little ballet slippers. I have somewhat shorter legs than my torso originally intended so I'm rarely out of my stiletto heels, but to my dismay, ballet slippers only come with flat soles and no heels. I was miserable with the lumpy look of my ankles, but I determined to persevere. (I had already paid for the lessons.)

I went to class the first night, but I quit after forty-five minutes. I mean, the slippers were bad enough, but the pink tights made my thighs look like two California redwood trees.

There was yet another rotten aspect to the exercises. (Oh, I know they called it *dancing,* but they didn't fool me. A plié is nothing more than a deep knee bend with a fancy French name.) In ballet, you have to exercise in front of a wall mirror. Have you ever seen your own reflection, broadside, when you're wearing nothing but pink tights, a leotard, ballet slippers, and visible panty lines? Dumbo, move over! If you weigh more than 90 pounds, I suggest you take several Valium before attempting such a depressing feat.

Next, I joined an **AEROBICS** class and, again, had another clothing crisis (tights with sneakers!). I worked through the warm-up, took my pulse, and headed for the door.

On my way home from that very class, I passed a movie house where *An Unmarried Woman* was showing. I was depressed from punking out on Aerobics so I bought a ticket and a pound of popcorn and sat down to watch Jill Clayburgh **JOGGING** up and down the Upper East Side and Soho. Boy, she looked great in sweat pants. I was inspired.

I jogged out of the movie theater; visions of Alan Bates dancing in my head.

I lasted a block and a half before I started experiencing serious lung pain. I was doubled over, breathing heavily, when I had a sudden revelation. I would have to abandon one of two activities: jogging or **SMOKING.**

I pondered the dilemma for ten seconds while I hailed a cab, jumped in, opened the window, and lit a cigarette. So much for jogging.

I gave **TENNIS** an intelligent evaluation by watching a Forest Hills match on television one afternoon. I concluded that, although it looked like fun to swing at the ball, there was far too much actual running involved with the game. It would be a fine sport for me if I could stand (or, better yet, sit) in one place and have the ball come to me. Similarly, I have the same problem with **RACQUETBALL, HANDBALL** or any other sport played with a bouncing ball.

I think **GOLF** is nice but the real drawback is you start playing very early in the morning (like at the crack of dawn), so that pretty well excludes me.

SWIMMING is as dangerous to the lungs as jogging so I avoid it at all costs, although I enjoy **DUNKING** on a hot summer afternoon.

I will concede that the great advantage to swimming is you don't have to worry about sweating. However, it is yet another sport that requires questionable attire.

GYMNASTICS is fun but not if you're older than four-and-a-half.

HORSEBACK RIDING develops inner thigh muscles you only need for sex and, given my sex life, it's not entirely necessary for me to be in such great shape.

BOWLING is too silly for serious consideration.

NAUTILUS EQUIPMENT is out of the question for the obvious reason that I'm far too intelligent to strap myself onto one of those horrible machines. Besides, **PASSIVE RESIST-ANCE** has never been my thing.

All in all, I think I gave a pretty fair shake to almost every available form of exercise. (I have the wardrobe to prove it.) Since nothing worked for me, I developed my own exercise program which I share with you in the following pages. Here is the first nonenergetic exercise program that is just right for you.

If, like me, you prefer to observe rather than participate in anything more strenuous than transporting the beer bottle from hand to mouth, I guarantee you've come to the right book.

Plain Jane's Fantasy   I would like to wake up one morning and discover that my dress size is the same number as my shoe size.

Preparations

1. Try not to set a regular time for exercising. Don't make this a consistent routine or the program may become habit-forming.

If you are a morning person (someone with lots of energy when you wake up), plan on exercising around midnight. Night people should set their alarm clocks for 6:15 A.M. when they are certain to sleep through it.

2. Call several friends before you start exercising. Leave urgent messages with all of them. Use whatever excuse comes to mind: fire, flood, police raid, unwanted pregnancy. Just make certain you emphasize the importance of an immediate reply.

The point is to make sure you will be interrupted by the telephone several times once you begin the exercises.

3. You will need a comfortable place for exercising. Some-place roomy and warm to avoid drafts. Your bed is perfect. The kitchen is also an excellent place to exercise but only after you've been to the food market and your refrigerator is well stocked. (See exercises for Arm Extensions.)

4. You will need an exercise mat, towel, or blanket for your floorwork. Your sofa will also work nicely and, if you happen to doze off, you're in the right place.

5. Dress for exercise. There is only one ironclad dress code you must follow. In order to get any benefit at all from this (or any exercise program), you absolutely must wear leg warmers, preferably several pair. Leotards, tights, sweat pants, tee shirts, unitards, jogging shorts, and sweat shirts are all optional as long as your calves are covered.

It is permissible to exercise naked but only from the knees up.

On days when you feel bloated, wear those loose-fitting parachute pants. Parachute pants hide a multitude of sins.

On days when you feel absolutely obese, wear the entire parachute.

Parachute available through the mail order division of Plain Jane Products, Inc.

6. A mirror is sometimes useful if available. It's always encouraging to check the position of your leg warmers as you work. (They should be bunched around the ankles at all times.)

7. Eat a full meal before beginning to exercise. Hopefully, this will make you too nauseated to continue working.

8. You will not need to visit your physician before you begin Plain Jane's exercise program. I guarantee you will not strain anything. This is because you will barely move anything.

MUSIC

Select a different record album for every set of exercises. Be careful to choose music that is most conducive to sitting still. This is a great incentive not to move. Look for albums that have very little rhythm or beat.

I highly recommend comedy albums by such artists as Robert Klein, George Carlin, or Richard Pryor.

An album such as *Richard Burton Recites The Spoon River Anthology* is doubly effective. You can't move to it, and it will probably put you to sleep anyway.

Also recommended are Kate Smith records and anything even vaguely patriotic.

If you have nothing but good music in your record collection, try playing your albums on a slower speed.

THE BURN

Expressions such as "feel the burn" and "make it burn" really make me burn. If you want to feel the burn, then smoke a pack of cigarettes. Otherwise, ban these expressions from your vocabulary.

If you do feel the burn, you are working much too hard. Slow down; stop and rest. You shouldn't feel anything even close to minor pain or you might actually see some results.

If you feel yourself getting warm, then it's time for a rest. If you start to sweat, take a two-day vacation.

WEIGHTS

As you advance in your exercise program, it may be

necessary to add small weights to your arms and legs. This will create greater resistance when the exercises become too easy for you. Personally, I prefer to use drumsticks for this purpose but only Kentucky Fried really works.

BREATHING

It is important to breathe while you work out. Also, at all other times.

I have included breathing hints with every exercise. My favorites are panting and heavy breathing, though not necessarily while exercising.

VITAMINS

I recommend Vitamin B_{52} for additional energy.

B_4 is usually better than after.

BEGINNER VS. ADVANCED

At the start of every new exercise program, you are faced with the embarrassment of entering a *beginner* class. Usually, the class is composed of either the very young, the very old, or the very uncoordinated.

On the other hand, if you go straight into an *advanced* class, chances are you will be nursing a charley horse for the next week-and-a-half.

Plain Jane has eliminated this problem. There are no beginner *or* advanced courses in my exercise program. All of my exercises are on the same level: *languid.*

INCREASING ENDURANCE

Exercise is like anything else in life. You must invest that extra effort to go the distance.

You need to push yourself to greater and greater heights. Constantly test yourself; try to surpass your own tough standards.

Every day I try to excel over the day before. Every night I concentrate my energies on the three most significant aspects of my life:

• **Sleeping.** I'm continually testing myself to determine just how many hours I can actually stay fast asleep. In 1976, my record was to sleep right through the Christmas holidays but this year I'm going for the whole month of December.

• **Eating ice cream.** In the Häagen-Dazs Marathon of Life, I am running in first place. Every evening I pack away as many pints as I can. I always go for that extra spoonful, no matter how nauseous it makes me.

• **Watching television.** I squeeze in more viewing time by turning on my television the moment I enter the house. Better yet, I try—as often as I can—to stay home all day and catch up on the soaps. In our house, we only turn off the TV during the news broadcasts; otherwise, we work hard to fill more and more of our time together with sitcoms and sporting events.

One word of caution: Do not be discouraged if you cannot achieve your goals in the beginning. All of us fall asleep during Johnny Carson at some time in our life.

Just give it your best effort. As my favorite folk hero always says, "Go for it." It's the eye of the tiger, Rocky.

Nutritional Information

1. For a well-balanced diet, you should select several different foods from the four essential food groups. At every meal, be sure to serve at least one food from each of the following categories:

White Bread

White Sugar

Soda Pop

Candy

Sugar, white bread, candy and soda pop available through the mail order division of Plain Jane Products, Inc.

2. Processed foods are also recommended for a well-balanced diet. There is no substitute for hot dogs and canned baked beans with plenty of ketchup.

3. Salt everything.

Carry a salt shaker in your purse in case of emergency. Eat plenty of the daily recommended dosage of high-sodium "P" foods: pretzels, potato chips, popcorn, and peanuts.

Avoid salt substitutes and saltpeter.

4. Most Americans eat over 130 pounds of sugar per year. Do not fall below your quota.

If you haven't eaten at least 65 pounds of sugar by midsummer, munch on sugar cubes until Christmas. (Be sure there is a dentist in your family; if not, marry one.)

5. If you must eat whole grain bread, be sure to negate its nutritional value with plenty of grape jelly.

6. Alcohol is high in calories and low in nourishment but, after the third martini, who cares?

Alcohol is a surefire appetite suppressant. If you drink enough liquor, chances are you will not have much craving for food.

7. Red meat is a great substitute for fish or chicken. Since cooking greatly reduces the fat content, learn to eat uncooked meat. Raw pot roast is a big favorite at our house.

8. High-fat food tastes better than low-fat. Use sour cream in place of yogurt.

9. Fruit is a basic element of any diet plan. Healthy and nutritious, fruit is naturally low in calories. But beware of raw fruit; it can be tainted.

Instead, substitute with baked fruit dishes such as blueberry muffins, strawberry shortcake, or banana cream pie. Remember that an apple a day keeps the doctor away, but so does an apple turnover.

Diet Tips

1. Don't substitute good nutrition for good taste.

2. Eliminate all green vegetables from your diet.

3. Keep plenty of nutritious snacks around the house. If you don't enjoy raw carrots, try Twinkies instead.

4. Eat only when you are really hungry, but try not to exceed thirteen or fourteen meals a day.

5. Teach your children about nutrition. Have them watch several hours of television every day. Commercials are particularly educational.
   Test your child's knowledge of sugary breakfast cereals. It's never too early to learn to love sugar.

6. Eat all your food while standing over the kitchen sink and staring at the electric clock. If you don't sit down to eat, it won't feel like a real meal.

7. Cook fattening meals for your family and friends. If everyone around you is gaining weight, you won't feel so fat yourself.

Dietary Supplements   Avoid all dietary supplements, especially those prepared in a blender. If you feel an urge for a protein drink, try an old-fashioned malted instead.

Sample Diet Plan

BREAKFAST
Coffee and cigarettes (unlimited quantity)

COFFEE BREAK
Coffee and Sweet 'N' Low
Sweet roll

LUNCH
One can of tuna fish (packed in water)
Two slices of whole wheat bread
One small jar of mayonnaise
Diet soda
Pickles (optional)
   or
One container of yogurt (because it's good for you)
One medium-sized brownie
   (as a reward for eating yogurt)

DINNER
Appetizer: Choose from your child's half-eaten
   hot dog or last night's cold spaghetti
Pistachio nuts (eat while cooking)
Red meat, raw or cooked
French fries (drain all oil)
Ketchup (unlimited quantity)
Dessert: Just a taste of chocolate ice cream

MIDNIGHT SNACK
Anything baked by Sara Lee

Ten Clever Ways to Lose Weight Without Dieting

Before you read any further, I must caution you that the following measures are extreme. My advice is to think twice before embarking on any of the techniques listed below. Although these measures have worked successfully for others, they can have troublesome side effects such as permanent brain damage and/or death.

However, I do know how it feels to be approaching your first pool party of the summer and still be carrying 20 pounds of winter's excess on your hips, so I present the following list as a public service to my readers.

1. The Jean Harris Diet Plan. Kill your lover. Spend several months on trial. Lose thirty pounds and get thirty years.

2. Dehydrate completely. Without any liquid in your system, you can reduce your total body weight to just under 27 pounds.

3. Become an Oriental person. It's a well-known medical fact that Chinese people are never overweight.

4. Give birth. Preferably to a baby. Guaranteed overnight weight loss.

5. Develop anorexia nervosa. This is especially effective if you are a teenage girl from a wealthy family. You will lose weight and drive your parents crazy at the same time.

6. Lapse into a coma. Remain comatose for an extended period of time. A steady diet of glucose will substantially reduce your body weight. (Also known as The Sunny Von Bulow Method.)

7. Increase your anxiety level. Use any of the following methods:
Getting married
Not getting married
Getting divorced
Not getting divorced

8. Grow a tapeworm. Visit a third world country and drink the water. Or, swallow a cassette.

9. Have major surgery. Any critical operation will do it. Unnecessary surgery is doubly effective.

10. Become a junkie. Drug addicts are generally able to maintain, or even lose, weight very easily.

Calorie Counting: The Round-Off-and-Subtract Method

Calorie Counting is one of the most ancient forms of weight reduction. It dates back even further than the discovery of Tab.

Personally, I think Calorie Counting is about as effective for dieting as the rhythm method is for birth control. I mean, with so many great diet pills on the market, why be bothered with counting calories?

However, I know a lot of people can't change their old habits so Calorie Counting will probably always be with us. Therefore, I offer the following suggestions to anyone still practicing this ancient method:

1. Try not to be too specific about the exact number of calories in any given food. Round off the numbers into general areas such as:

Under 50 calories: water, coffee, celery.

Between 100 and 500 calories: cottage cheese, yogurt, fruit, a glass of wine, half a Twinkie.

Over 1000 calories: anything worth eating in the first place.

2. Don't panic until your daily caloric intake exceeds the five figure mark.

3. Subtract the calories your system burns through physical activities. Be sure to account for every movement of your body, including breathing.

4. Never buy a calorie counter book unless you are prepared for the worst.

5. If you expect to remain popular, never remind a friend of the caloric value of the chocolate cake she is eating.

Plain Jane's Favorite Fad Diets

I know fad diets are dangerous. I know they can damage my health. I know I'm only losing water. I know I'll gain back every ounce (and then some) the moment I go off the diet. But I can't help myself. With me, it's either feast or famine, literally.

In line at the supermarket—my basket filled with cottage cheese and Entenmann's—I can't resist sneaking a peek at the Enquirer article promising I can lose 30 pounds *while I sleep!* I mean, you never know when you'll get lucky and hit a diet that really works.

These are among my very favorites:

1) Eat only at certain times:
   a) Diet all week and gorge yourself on weekends.
   b) Eat every other day.
   c) Eat only in months with the letter "R" in them.

2) Before each meal eat (or drink) one of the following:
   a) A grapefruit   c) An apple
   b) A glass of water d) Kryptonite

3) At every meal, eat only one kind of food:
   a) High protein   c) Italian
   b) Carbohydrate

4) Eat only in:
   a) Scarsdale   b) Beverly Hills

5) Only buy diet books with cute titles:
   a) I Love New York Diet
   b) I Love America Diet
   c) I Ate Chicago Diet

For further information, refer to Plain Jane's two books on diet and nutrition: *Plain Jane Eats Out* and *Plain Jane Pigs Out.*

Eye patches available through the mail order division of Plain Jane Products, Inc.

Tips for Exercise Class

1. Stay home.

2. If you must attend, arrive a half hour late. Be sure to miss the warm-ups so that you can gently limber up while the rest of the class does jumping jacks.

3. Stand next to the fattest woman in class. Watch her in the mirror and remind yourself things could always be worse.

4. Work in the back of the room. You don't want anyone to select *you* as the fattest woman in class.

5. Select an exercise teacher who speaks a foreign language, preferably Japanese or Russian. Hopefully, you won't understand a word of her instructions and you can spend most of the hour raising your hand and asking questions.

6. Try to catnap between exercises. This is especially easy in yoga class, but be sure not to start snoring.

7. Never lie on your tummy if the health club is carpeted. The smell from health club carpets is enough to make you faint.

8. During calisthenics, try not to spit at the instructor. Save the abusive language for your friends, family, and lovers.

9. After class, reward yourself for doing your exercises. Have a pizza.

Plain Jane's Dial-an-Exercise   For a small weekly fee, you can call our telephone number (no collect calls, please!) and hear Plain Jane instruct an entire exercise class in less than three minutes.

Plain Jane's Join-Up™

Plain Jane's JOIN-UP™ Health Clubs are opening this year in many cities across the country.

It's so easy to become a member of JOIN-UP™. Just find the JOIN-UP™ Studio in your hometown and give us a call. (You won't even have to come down to see us. We'll make all the arrangements over the phone.)

You'll pay an enormous membership fee. You'll select a personalized exercise regimen from our extensive range of classes, and then you'll never bother to show up.

For an additional charge, JOIN-UP™ will hire an energetic high school student to attend classes and exercise for you.***

If you can't find one of Plain Jane's JOIN-UP™ Studios in your hometown, why not join one in a neighboring state? Think how easy it will be, not to attend class, when your health club is 753 miles away from home.

***When ordering a student, please specify how often you would exercise if you had the time, energy, or inclination. Our students are available once a week, once a month, and once in a blue moon.

THE EXERCISES

WARM-UPS: Getting Into Your Tights

Purpose: To overheat yourself and ruin a brand-new pair of tights at the same time. (NOTE: Brand-new stockings may be substituted.)

Music: Any Italian Opera

Starting Position: Barefoot.

1. Slip feet into tights.

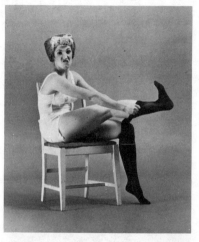

2. Pull tights above knees, using whatever strength required.

3. Change positions if necessary.

4. Puncture tights beyond repair.

Breathing: Exasperated.

WARM-UPS: For the Very, Very Lazy

Purpose: To stimulate your cardiovascular system and increase the circulation of your blood without moving a single muscle in your body.
  Select one or more of the following exercises.

Music: Hum quietly to yourself

Starting Position: Slightly chilled.

1. Wearing a warm jacket or overcoat, stand in front of a kerosene space heater. (NOTE: A roaring fire or steam-heat radiator will also work.)

Kerosene Space Heater available through the mail order division of Plain Jane Products, Inc.

2. Polish off the remains of a brandy bottle.

3. Recline underneath a sun lamp. If this exercise is too easy for you, increase the difficulty by using a sun reflector.

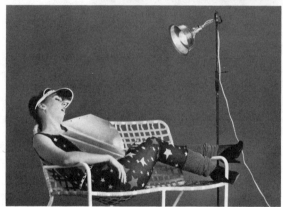

4. Be amorous; kiss a sailor.

Breathing: Sniff brandy. Breathe through your nose during heavy necking.

WARM-UPS: Aerobics (Jogging)

Purpose: Every warm-up should include a series of aerobic exercises. Aerobics speed up your pulse rate and make your heart work harder. Unfortunately, this can lead to heavy perspiration.

   After many hours of exhaustive research, I have discovered the secret to painless Aerobics. No, it's not deep breathing. It's sitting down.

Music: The Watergate Tapes

Starting Position: Sit in your favorite chair, feet together, shoulders slightly slouched.

1. Lift left leg several inches off the floor.

2. Lift right leg several inches off floor as you lower left leg. Repeat steps 1 and 2 for 20 counts. Stop and rest if you feel tired.

3. Turn chair and repeat entire exercise on other side.

Breathing: Inhale when lifting left leg; exhale when lifting right leg. Hold breath when moving chair.

Chair available through the mail order division of Plain Jane Products, Inc.

ARMS: The Refrigerator Lunge

Purpose: Arm exercises are important to strengthen and tone the upper arm flab that jiggles whenever you wear summer clothes. Of course, the simple alternative is to burn every sleeveless shirt in your wardrobe.

Music: Food Glorious Food

Starting Position: Hungry.

1. Extend right arm; firmly clasp refrigerator handle.

2. Twist body towards refrigerator and pull door.

3. Lunge into refrigerator. Inspect every food item and select only the least nutritious and most fattening treat. Take your time; the cold air is an excellent beauty treatment for your skin.

Breathing: Cold enough to see your breath.

WAIST: Full Body Lift

Purpose: To hang suspended in mid-air.

Music: Learn to Type in Ten Easy Lessons

Starting Position: Lie on right side with legs extended.

1. Friend lifts your legs and then lowers them to the floor. Repeat five times. Release legs.

2. Another friend lifts your arms. Lowers them. Repeat five times. (NOTE: Leg warmers should be transferred to arms for this and any other arm exercise.)

3. Both friends, at the count of three, hoist you above the floor. Hold for fifteen minutes, or until one of your friends passes out. Release.

Breathing: Provide canisters of oxygen to relieve friends.

WAIST: The Killer Stretch

Purpose: The Killer Stretch is twenty-five years in Sing-Sing. It is especially effective when used in connection with *The Jean Harris Diet Plan* (see page 22).

Music: Jailhouse Rock

Starting Position: Innocent until proven guilty.

1. Pivot left. Hands on waist.

2. Pivot right. Think about the Scarsdale Diet Doctor.

3. Lunge forward.

Breathing: Inhale, exhale, growl.

ABDOMINALS

Warning To Reader: Abdominal exercises are dangerous to your health and well-being. There is no easy way to do a sit-up.

Therefore, Plain Jane suggests you never attempt to exercise this area of your anatomy.

Adamantly refuse to do abdominal work. Scratch the abdominal exercises from your exercise records, rip them from your books, tear them from your cassettes, pound them out of your video tapes.

It is your right (indeed, your duty) to protest cruel and inhumane exercise routines.

LEG LIFTS

Purpose: To placate my stepmother, who begged and pleaded to be in my book.

It was against my better judgment to include her (she is *months* older than any of my other models, or myself).

In this series of photographs, I'm helping Stepmom demonstrate the proper method for leg lifts.

Music: Cast recording, The Taming of the Shrew

Starting Position: Marry for money.

1. Raise leg a few inches off the floor.

2. Lift leg to hip level or as high as possible without straining muscles.

3. Helping Stepmom feel the burn.

Breathing: Knock the wind out of anyone under 107 pounds.

LEGS: Tendon Stretch

Purpose: To strengthen, tone and firm the muscles you will need to walk in high heels.

Music: NASA Moonwalk Tapes

Starting Position: Buy the sexiest pair of stiletto high heels you can find.

1. Reach for the ceiling.

2. Bend over and touch heels.

3. Walk forward.

4. Perform Yoga stretch.

5. React immediately if you hear an exercise instructor.

Breathing: Yes.

BUTTOCK LIFTS

Purpose: To get a cheap thrill.

Music: Moon Over Miami

Starting Position: Flabby.

1. The buttock lift is a very subtle movement. Learn to feel the squeeze.

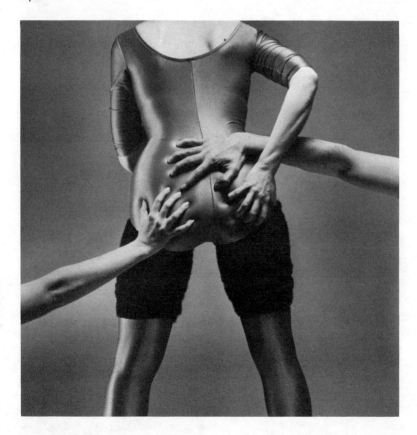

2. Lie on floor. Rest your weight on your shoulders, lift buttocks.

3. Side view of Step 2 (above). It is okay to get all the help you need. (You may also use pillows if telephone books are too heavy for you to lift.)

Breathing: Discreetly clear your throat for buttock squeeze.

COOL DOWN

Purpose: To end your exercise routine.

Music: Sounds of Niagara Falls

Starting Position: Exhausted and vulnerable.

1. Inhale and raise arms.

2. Exhale and lower arms.

3. Duck!

Breathing: Hold breath under water.

Plastic bucket available through the mail order division of Plain Jane Products, Inc.

SPECIAL EXERCISES:
Isometrics

Purpose: Isometrics offer an excellent method of exercising without having to attend classes. You can perform Isometrics almost anywhere. Here, Plain Jane demonstrates the proper technique for performing Isometrics while waiting on line in her local supermarket.

Remember that these exercises can also be done while standing in line at the movie theater, while riding the bus to work in the morning or in any elevator.

Music: Muzak

Starting Position: Bored.

1. Jumping Jacks while unloading shopping basket.

2. Side stretch with groceries.   *Breathing:* Alot

SPECIAL PROBLEMS:
Back Pains

Quite often, our emotional problems manifest themselves in physical discomfort. I often feel as though I am carrying the weight of the world on my shoulders.

For instance, my current Stepmom is a real pain in my neck, back and other unmentionable parts of my anatomy.

Unfortunately, many of my readers may have to shoulder similar family burdens. My remedy is a daily dose of Grin-and-Bear-It. Happily for me, it's only a matter of time; Daddy's marriages never last for very long.

Plain Jane Weighs In

Recently, a gorgeous (if you like the type), blonde, blue-eyed model published her first beauty book. I can't mention her name but her initials are C.T. (seriously).

In her book, C.T. tells us how to determine our ideal weight. Her formula is simple:

> 100 pounds for your first 5 feet
> Add 3 pounds for every inch over 5 feet

For example, say you are 5'1" (like me). According to C.T., I should weigh 103 pounds.

Well, I haven't seen 103 since my last high fever. But, on the other hand, what does a high fashion model know about real life? And, how can you trust anyone with a body like Cheryl Tiegs? (Oops!)

Listen to Plain Jane. Here's my realistic weight chart for Large-framed women:***

> 100 pounds for the first 4 feet
> Add 10 pounds for every inch over 4 feet

My 5'1" woman will feel much more at ease with herself. Like myself, she may even find herself slightly underweight and, therefore, entitled to a rich dessert for dinner tonight.

***Large-framed means you do, indeed, have bones.

Tipping the Bathroom Scale in Your Favor

Every once in a while, it is necessary to weigh yourself. I am fully aware of how painful this prospect can be. However, there are a few tricks for easing the transition from bathroom floor to bathroom scale.

1. Set your bathroom scale for 10 pounds underweight. Erase this deed from your mind.

2. Slide the scale along the bathroom floor until you find the correct position, preferably resting uphill on the bathroom mat.

3. Tentatively place one foot on the scale. If you don't like what you see, jump off at once.

4. Never let the dial settle on one number. Keep it moving by shifting your weight back and forth. Jump off the scale when the dial is on the downswing.

5. Clutch the sink the entire time you are weighing yourself.

6. If you are unhappy with the general area where the dial hovers, convince yourself the scale is off by five pounds (possibly more).

7. Balance yourself on the balls of your feet. Never allow your heels to touch the scale.

8. Always deduct at least two pounds for water retention.

9. If you are dressed while weighing yourself, subtract the following amounts:
   skirt or slacks — ½ pound
   jeans — ¾ pound
   blouse — ½ pound; 2 pounds (sweat shirt with shoulder pads)
   underwear and stockings — ¼ pound

socks — ¼ pound per foot
shoes — 3 pounds (flats); 3½ pounds (high heels)
boots — 4 pounds
barrettes, hair pins — ¼ pound
makeup — ¼ pound
nail polish — ¼ pound (fingers); ¼ pound (toes)

(NOTE: In some cases, it may be advisable to get fully dressed before weighing yourself.)

10. If you are completely naked, deduct two pounds for bodily hair and dental work.

11. Remove your eyeglasses or contact lenses. They add additional weight and, without them, you can't see the numbers on the dial.

12. Never purchase a doctor's scale. Buy the cheapest bathroom scale you can find. Look for one that only goes up to 115 pounds.

I'm Beautiful, You're Beautiful: It's the Law!

As you all know, Plain Jane is an activist. Part of my basic function in life is to voice my opinions about everything.

I enjoy being actively involved in politics. My family and I like to tour the country, making whistle-stop speeches.

I am working to support the passage of the "I'm Beautiful, You're Beautiful" law, currently being debated in the California legislature.

The IBYB law would make it perfectly legal (even preferable) for every woman in America to be ten to fifteen pounds overweight. Fat jokes would be outlawed. It would be illegal to say the following words to any woman: "You have such a pretty face, if only you'd lose weight."

Severe penalties would be imposed on anyone caught dieting while on vacation or during the Christmas holidays.

Under IBYB guidelines, it will be mandatory for every woman over 30 to own three complete wardrobes. We classify these wardrobes as:

- **Old reliable.** Clothes that fit your current size.
- **Oh boy, I'm in trouble if these pants fit me.** Your barometer for determining when you've gone overboard with the pasta and beer.
- **Those were the days.** This, your most cherished wardrobe, once fit you (only once, several years ago, for about a week). You probably purchased this wardrobe while on the final leg of a three-week water and lettuce diet.

IBYB will prohibit a woman from wearing a tight pair of slacks to remind herself how fat she has gotten and how she shouldn't stuff her face at dinner. All overeating will be done on a mandatory basis.

Supporters of IBYB have unanimously agreed to include the "No Guilt" rider that has been totally misinterpreted by the "Right-to-Diet" coalition. "No Guilt" only means that every time you feel guilty about your weight, you are entitled to a free banana split (paid for by your mother).

Exercises of Extreme Cruelty will be outlawed from the land on a federal level and locally enforced by state officials. Extremely cruel exercises include touching your toes and, most explicitly, any variation on hip exercises. In addition, certain incredibly difficult sports will be banned, including any activity that requires bare upper thighs or pink tights.

I urge you to get involved with our struggle. Support IBYB! These are your flabby upper arms we are defending! Write to your senators, your governors, your congresspersons! We lost ERA, let's not lose IBYB!

Selected Items from Plain Jane's Catalog

I don't have a box number yet, but when I do, you can send a check or money order to *Plain Jane Products, Inc.* for any of the following items:

"I ♥ Plain Jane" tee shirt (Adult/large sizes only)........ $12.95

"Mom Worked Out With Plain Jane But All I Got Was This Lousy Tee Shirt" tee shirt (Child's sizes)....................... $12.95

"No Sweat" Sweat Shirt... $12.95

"No Sweat" Sweat Bands $12.95/pair

Plain Jane Poster in various sizes:
Wallet Size.......... $12.95
Book Size........... $12.98
Wall Size $12.98
Billboard Size $11,112.98
Autographed (by my husband because I'm too busy) Edition...................Add $12.95

PLAIN JANE WORKS OUT on a long-playing record $12.95
PLAIN JANE WORKS OUT on a cassette $12.98
PLAIN JANE WORKS OUT on video tape $49.98
PLAIN JANE WORKS OUT on 16mm film $112.95
PLAIN JANE WORKS OUT in wallet-sized photos (set of 32 photographs) $12.95
PLAIN JANE WORKS OUT on computer print-out $49.98
The PLAIN JANE WORKS OUT Video Arcade Game . . $2,049.98
The Portable Home Version $49.98

"I Felt the Burn" ash trays. $12.95
"Down With the Burn" beer mugs $12.95
"Ban the Burn" Placards (suitable for strikes and demonstrations). $12.95

Membership Fee in Plain Jane's JOIN-UP™ club . . . . Prices vary per state but anticipate the worst

Plain Jane (or an authorized unemployed actress) comes to your house and watches you try to exercise. $249.95 per half hour visit

PLAIN JANE NEWSLETTER. . . . . . $49.95 per year
DIAL-AN-EXERCISE . . . . $2.95 per call

Plain Jane Doll—"The first full-fashion doll with cellulite" $49.95

"Honk If You Worked Out With Plain Jane" Bumper Sticker $12.95
"Support IBYB" buttons $12.95/dozen
Plain Jane's dual-purpose Exercise Mat and Sleeping Bag. . . $49.98

Free Copy of ITEMS FROM PLAIN JANE'S CATALOG includes banners, pennants, postcards, tote bags, coffee mugs, platters, leotards, tights, full-harness parachutes, leg warmers, arm bands, and much much more. . . $12.95 (for postage and handling)

Recommended Reading

Ellen Shirley Brownnose. *Losing It All.*
Bess Fryerson. *I Love Miss America Diet.*
Garfield. *Jim Davis Gains Weight.*
Doc George Hehan. *Running and Bingeing.*
Leo Jetcaglia. *Living, Loving and Learning to Lose Weight.*
Judy Mazel-tov. *I Bought Beverly Hills Diet.*
Richard Wholegrain Millhouse Nixon. *The Cottage Cheese and Ketchup Diet.*
Jean M. Owl. *Recipes From The Cave Bear.*
Plain Jane. *Thin Skin In Thirty Days.*
Judith Prantz. *Mistral's Menu.*
Victoria Princesspal. *The TV Dinner Diet.*
Mister Spock. *Baby Fat And Child Care.*
Stillman's Water Torture Diet.
Suzanne Summers. *Ode To A Diet: An Anthology of Low-Calorie Poetry.*
Elizabeth Tinker-Taylor-Soldier-Sailor. *I Loved Washington Diet.*
Harold S. Tushner. *When Fattening Things Happen to Skinny People.*
Barbara Wawa. *Interview With Three Fat People and Cher.*
Janet Weekly. *That Calder Diet.*

Plain Jane Newsletter   For a small monthly fee, we will mail you our latest update on Plain Jane's current projects, movies, guest appearances on television and picket line, plus her pet gripe of the month.

A Final Word...

No beauty book by Plain Jane would be complete if it didn't conclude with an interminable, but sincere, discussion of nuclear proliferation, pollution, chemical waste, corporate control of America, the hazards of asbestos, Love Canal, and petrochemicals (whatever they are).

However, lack of space in this slim volume and the narrow-mindedness of my editor prohibits the inclusion of the above topics. For the moment, it will suffice to say that I am against most of these things.

Interested readers will be able to study a more detailed statement of my views in my forthcoming book, *Plain Jane Speaks Out.* In addition to discussing my previous involvement with international politics, *Plain Jane Speaks Out* will include the latest scientific advances in nail-wrapping and the removal of unsightly facial hair.

After exercising with Plain Jane,
eat a nourishing meal and take a long nap.
You deserve it!